NOREEN MCCLENDON

Living Authentically You

Five Steps To Personal Peace

DEDICATION
This book is dedicated to Yahweh for giving me words to express
HIS infinite wisdom.

Contents

Introduction

Five Steps To Personal Peace Living Authentically You

There are times in your life when things seem to happen out of nowhere. When you least expect them to happen. When you don't know which way to turn. When you are excited, scared and giddy with the possibilities all at the same time.

It is in these moments when it is critical to have a way to filter out the emotional noise and figure out:

1) what you feel

2) why you feel what you do

3) what is your bottom line

4) what you are going to do or not do

5) set your time limit; and

1

6) get the answers to these questions without emotion.

Emotions are real. They rise up when we are under pressure. They also cloud our judgment and have been the foundation of some very poor choices. Choices that lead to outcomes we didn't want and didn't serve us in the long run.

The goal is to come out on the other end of the experience with the best possible outcome for YOU and with peace of mind. There are five simple steps that you must take to ensure that you come out of any experience with the best possible outcome for you.

The five steps are:

1. Know yourself
2. Determine your position
3. Verbalize your position/needs/expectations/desires/boundaries
4. Watch the behavior of others
5. Do what is in your best interest

In this book, I will detail the steps laid out to me by my Creator, Yahweh, in the midst of a situation that was charged with emotions, hopes, desires and lots of potential to go extremely well or extremely bad. Follow me as I share the five steps that can be used in any situation. It has since been revealed to me that these steps apply to any situation. They are not restricted to the type of situation I was facing.

The five steps that will force you to be honest with yourself about what you want and why. These five steps will lead you to living an authentic life. No longer will you make life's many decisions based on circumstance, but principles.

The key is that decisions be made based on the "principle at play." in any situation. Often, we make decisions based on the needs, desires of others, appearances, fear of not being liked, fear of not fitting in (and this isn't relegated to teenage peer pressure – adults still do it every day) , and fear of losing a relationship or position in our careers. All of these reasons, and more, cause us to move further away from who we really are and want to be and toward a fake, chaos-filled existence. This is the opposite of being authentically you.

When you finish this book, you will have a blueprint that works in EVERY situation. This is not a guarantee that you will get everything you want in life or suddenly become invincible and incapable of being hurt. But what you WILL come out of this ride with is a pattern to follow that will minimize devastation in every situation.

More often than not, you will be comfortable and at peace with the choices you made because they will have been made based on your principles, your values, and what you believe , and based on the information available to you at that time , with regard to what you truly believe is best. Sometimes, what you want is not always going to be the best decision. This is where the principle at play becomes invaluable to the choices before you.

In the book "Seven Habits Of Highly Effective People," Steven Covey writes about leading a "principle-centered" life. If you center your life on in anything other than principles, it is less likely that you will be fulfilled. in your life. It is likely that you will be tossed around with every change.

Your life will be shifting in ways that you don't choose, but rather, the shifting nature of the "thing" you center your life around. For example, if you center your life on money, your happiness, contentment, and joy will all be subject to the state of your money.

If it is centered on your mate, the state of your relationship with your mate will determine the state of your happiness, contentment and joy. You will make decisions solely to feed whatever you center your life around. You become, by accident almost, dependent on things you can't control to make you feel valuable, content, happy, joyful and successful.

I have to caution you, however. Putting these steps in place may cause some people to be angry with you. I say – fuck 'em. Yup. Fuck 'em. I would much rather someone else be mad – while having no choice but to respect my get down – than for ME to be mad.

Maybe it's just me, but that's how I'm rolling. I'm going to live my truth. I'm going to tell you what I need. I'm going to serve the principles I believe to be right based on the information I have. I'm going to set my boundaries and hold fast to them. If I don't, I am teaching others that it is acceptable to disregard them.

4

Introduction

I intend to live being authentically me. I may not have very many friends when it's over, but the ones I have will be true blue. They will be ride-or-die. They will be those things because they know the real me. They won't one day wake up and find I have drifted away from my character into someone they didn't sign up to ride with. I will be honest with those around me. I will be at peace with my choices. My hope is that once you learn and understand these five basic steps, you too will live your life in a way that best serves your needs.

This is not a book to teach you how to be self-centered and an asshole. It is designed to show you how to stand up for your principles and values. These are seemingly invisible things but are THE VERY THINGS THEMSELVES.

Principles are the true substance, the things you can hang your hat on.

KNOW YOURSELF

The most important knowledge anyone can have is "knowledge of self. ". It is vital to know yourself, strengths/weaknesses, limitations, flaws and all. It is the most important relationship you have. If you don't know yourself, you are subject to other people's version of who and what you should be. You cannot be authentic, because you are motivated by things, people and circumstances **you can't control**.

There is a saying: "If you don't know where you're going other people will be too happy to tell you where to go." There is another saying: "If you don't stand for something, you will fall for anything." These sayings have circulated through time because they are true "principles.".

This writing will focus heavily on "principles.". Therefore, it is critical that we have use the same language and understanding of what principles are. Here is the Merriam Webster's definition of principle: a **comprehensive and fundamental law,** doctrine or assumption; **a rule or code of conduct**; habitual **devotion to right** principles; the laws or facts of nature underlying the working of an artificial device.

When we discuss principles in this book, we will be speaking from the definitions in bold above: a comprehensive and fundamental law and rule or code of conduct and a devotion to right principles. All of these are PERSONAL TO YOU. Specifically, we are talking about the comprehensive and fundamental laws that you live by. If you don't have any, you MUST develop them. If you don't stand for something, you will fall for anything. The rules or code of conduct by which you live your life are what we are focusing on. Again, if you don't have any, you MUST develop a set.

If you search your heart and find that you don't have any fundamental laws, code of conduct or devotion to right that you will not violate or allow anyone else to violate, do not despair. Many people do not.

However, if you are to live an authentic life, one that is centered in principles, it is necessary to develop them. It will require you to have an honest conversation with yourself about what is truly important to you and why.

The "why" is where the most work will be necessary on the journey to self-discovery. Think of how small children learn. They ask you a question. You answer. They ask you why. You answer. They ask why again. You answer. They ask why again. You answer. This can go on for several rounds until they are satisfied that they fully understand or you get frustrated and tell them "because!" ! That is how detailed you have to be with yourself to get to your **comprehensive and fundamental law**.

I will give you an example. I thought for a long time that it made me angry when a man would tell me he was going to call and didn't. I certainly felt intense feelings about it.

When I asked myself why, I thought it was because it was disrespectful. Why did I think disrespectful? If I thought it was disrespectful, why am I angry?. Why don't I simply not engage in a relationship with this man?

When I continued to ask myself "why," , it uncovered the truth of my discontent. The truth is that it hurts my feelings. What I feel is hurt, not anger.

I am hurt because I PERCEIVE it to mean that I AM NOT IMPORTANT ENOUGH TO THE PERSON TO FOLLOW THROUGH WITH THEIR COMMITMENT TO CALL. OK, that is way different than just being angry. That speaks to how I feel about myself, and what insecurity that act triggers in me. It also requires me to acknowledge that the other person's behavior may have nothing at all to do with what I PERCEIVE it to be. It is my own insecurities that are at play and causing me pain. This requires total honesty with myself.

In my book *HURT PEOPLE HIGHWAY, Identifying Unhealthy Elements In Relationships*, I write about the hardest day of my life

8

being the day I had to look at myself in the mirror and accept that the reason I was in so much pain related to a relationship was MY FAULT.

What? You mean I set myself up for this intense pain. Yes! I did that to myself. Why? Because I did not have a **code of conduct** that governed my behavior and set boundaries for how my partner treated me. Why? Because in my relationship with my father, I always felt that if I didn't do the work to maintain the relationship bond, he would walk away.

I carried that insecurity into all relationships with men. It was the source of all the actions I took that led me to devastation in relationships. There is no way to engage in a relationship of any kind without the **fundamental laws** and **devotion to right/laws** that will govern my behavior in that relationship. I don't get to control other people, only myself.

This is the process of asking "why" that led me to the real reason. It uncovered things about me. In this process, it is critical to focus on your own behavior and Feelings.

Remember, this is about knowing you, not knowing the other person. That will never lead you to your principles. It is also a distraction that people use to avoid checking themselves and their own bullshit. Check yourself before you begin to check others.

Here is another example. My non-profit has a contract with another non-profit to provide three people to perform certain services. I pay in advance and get reimbursed the following month. The company did not pay in 2 two months. That meant four paychecks to three people that were not fundamental to my business.

This was truly a "public benefit" arrangement. My company was not earning any money. We were simply a pass-through to the workers and provided supervision. The other company was having internal shifting and could not get the checks signed. For my company, the bottom line, the **fundamental law,** was that we would not incur any additional outlay of cash unless we were paid for what was already spent. It didn't matter what the consequences were to the other company, the employees or the community.

We did not have any more money to spend without being reimbursed. It was not an emotional decision. It was based on the **fundamental law** of our bank account that we simply could not afford to carry three employees without a source to pay them. I could not risk the salaries of the essential employees trying to do a good thing for the three workers or the community. I also was not willing to have the three employees work and not pay them. That would have been unethical.

As a responsible executive, I had to make the company's position known to the client, establish a timeline and , wait to see if they performed and responded. I wasn't in a position to care if they liked me anymore. I wasn't in a position to be concerned about how anyone felt. It wasn't personal. I AM responsible for the fiscal health of the company that I am employed by.

By understanding the bottom line of the company, the choices before me became crystal clear. If I had included in the decision-making process how others would be affected, I surely would have had a lot harder choice to make. If, for one second, I let the families of the three employees enter into my decision, it would have made my hard line stance much more difficult to achieve.

My heart would ache at the idea that they would not have income. I would be up at night concerned about whether the families would have food to eat. If I ever allowed my personal feelings or emotions to enter into the decision-making process, my choices would have been less clear. I would have been trying to balance the damage to the families with the competing interests of the company. It certainly would have kept me up for a few nights. Since I was able to remove the emotions, personal feelings and the interests of others that were not "the company," I was able to determine what choices were actually available. I presented them to the client and they responded.

There was no need for a big confrontation. This was not about blame. It was simply a statement of what the company was prepared to do, what we were not able or willing to take on and what we would do if they did not respond. It was not necessary for me to control the other company's actions. It was simply my job to know what my company's position was, verbally express that to the other company, wait on their actions and respond in the best interests of the company that for which I am legally, financially and ethically responsible to. As a dear friend of mine says often: "Easy call.".

Knowing yourself boils down to understanding the bottom line for you, your family, your company or whatever entity you for which you are making a decision for. If you remove emotions, the potential impact on others (as crazy as that sounds) and old fears and insecurities from the equation and focus only on your **fundamental law, code of conduct and devotion to right**, your choices will narrow and you will be able to make the main thing the main thing. You will find that what you should do in any situation becomes clear to you. Its like the path becomes crystal clear. The more competing interests you remove from the equation, the clearer your choices will become and it will be easier to make those choices, despite the way others feel about your decision.

These experiences will leave you with a peace that no one can take from you. It will cause you to employ the practice more often because of how it impacts you. It will be uncomfortable during the process because most of us are socialized to believe that if we are focusing on our needs first and only, that we are being selfish. That is true. Selfishness has a negative connotation.

Well, I have discovered that I needed to be selfish and that there is a difference between selfish and self-centered. Remember, whatever you "center" your life on will determine your joy. If we are self-centered, everything we focus on will be about us. It does not allow room to think of others at all. That is where a righteous principle crosses the line into a perverted, negative space. I don't know about you, but I can create drama sitting in a room all by myself. How do I do that? I make assumptions about the motives of others. I let my insecurities tell me that someone is disrespecting me.

The truth is NONE of those things **have** to be true. It doesn't mean I won't get worked up about them. It doesn't mean I won't get angry about them. So for me, I would rather be principle-centered than ME-centered. It does not mean that I should not be "selfish.".

Focus first on you. Spend time learning what motivates and inspires you, what angers, hurts and upsets you. Examine the difference between what you say you want and what you respond to, accept and participate in. This alone is an eye-opening exercise. Learn how to identify things that have been traumatic that have left scars and that cause you to react or perceive the motives of others without proof or confirmation that those perceptions are true or real. In short, get to know and acknowledge your baggage.

You carry it everywhere you go and into every situation. You might as well understand it and not let it derail your hopes and dreams. Recognize that you are responsible to manage your baggage. It is not the responsibility of people that you are in relationships with (business or personal) to navigate your baggage. It is not other people's responsibility to know, understand and adjust to your insecurities, flaws and post-trauma stress.

Those things are your responsibility. The only way to do that is to acknowledge that they exist. If someone chooses to adjust to your baggage, it is because they choose to and a gift usually borne out of love for you – not obligation or responsibility. Cherish it and do your part to minimize the hard work required to work through someone else baggage.

13

Don't use it as a crutch to continue behaving irrationally, hyper-sensitively and overly reactionary. Reminds me of a church saying: God says come as you are. . .but it doesn't mean you stay that way. Meaning if you attend any spiritual services on a regular basis and you are still walking around with the same baggage you had when you arrived at that house of worship/spiritual center, you are in the wrong place or you are not practicing the lessons being taught.

Remember, the only expert on you is you. Nobody can decide what will work for you or set your boundaries.Nobody knows your needs or expectations if you don't tell them. You alone are responsible for the state and condition of your emotional and physical condition. Even if you have been the victim of a horrific trauma, you still control how long you will allow the trauma to affect your life moving forward.

You are the captain of your ship, the star in the movie that is your life. You just have to know how you want it to play out and what you want the ending (outcome of any exchange) to be.

STEP 1 TAKEAWAYS

1. When important decisions need to be made, identify the principle at play that will guide your decision.
2. You MUST develop a comprehensive and fundamental law, doctrine or assumption; a rule or code of conduct; habitual devotion to right (principles) for yourself or whatever entity for which you are making a decision.
3. It is required to be totally honest about your reasons, good or bad. It is required to be honest about the interests of the entity you are making the decision for - no matter how the other party will feel or react. You get to the principles by asking a series of "why" questions.
4. Being principle-centered allows you to focus on keeping "the main thing the main thing." You need to do an honest assessment of yourself, including, strengths, weaknesses,

flaws, traumas and any other baggage you have so that as you evaluate any situation, you are conscious of how your baggage is influencing your thoughts.

5. Nobody is responsible for your baggage but you. If they choose to adjust themselves to accommodate your baggage it is because it is their choice and likely comes from a place of love. You are the only expert on you.

DETERMINE YOUR POSITION

Since I was shown this five-step process for making decisions, every decision is easier to make. My choices come to me faster. I don't waffle. I also come out the other end of uncomfortable situations at peace with the choice I made.

I am able to live authentically. I determine what my position is (based on the principle at play) and focus on that. Everything else is just noise. I have found that my emotions and the emotions of others play a smaller role in the decisions made.

This is important because emotions are not necessarily based in fact. Nor are they always relevant to the situation at hand. Emotions can be triggered by past experiences that have no bearing on the current dilemma. In those instances, they become a hindrance. In fact, they can become destructive to the process.

17

To determine your position, you must be honest with yourself. It requires you to evaluate your needs/expectations/limitati ons/boundaries/capacity to perform and/or what you want. The more attention paid to these realities, the more likely it is that your position will become clear. However, there will be times when you begin the process thinking one position is best, but upon further review of the situation, you determine that another position will better serve you and everyone involved.

It is important here to say that even if other people who are directly or indirectly affected by your position don't like it, it is always best that they are given the respect and dignity of knowing what it is. They don't have to like it, but they will have no choice but to respect it and you. As a person who would rather be respected than loved, I will take that outcome every day of the week.

Often when we are faced with a decision, there are things involved that are not said or seem unrelated that influence the situation. For me, I have found that when I experience great loss, like the death of my parents and oldest brother, I have experienced depressions.

I may not consciously know that I am depressed, but I figured out that a telltale sign of me being depressed is the cleanliness of my house. I can walk around the house and every room will have something out of place. I have also found that once I clean things up, I feel better emotionally. The two don't seem related, but they influence each other, in my experience.

Recently, I was faced with a decision involving a man that I am in love with, had a previous relationship with, want to be with but who has not been consistent in my life and I did not want to be hurt by. I very much wanted to help him, but did not want to be used.

I had to be honest with myself about what fundamental law was in play, what right principle I was devoted to and what MY code of conduct was going to be. I could not control the conduct of the man. I could only control (if I was lucky - due to my emotional attachment and previous insecurities) my conduct. It took me between 24 and 48 hours to get to the bottom of those things.

I discovered, after all of my "why" questions, that my fundamental laws were these:

1) I wanted to have a relationship with this man if it was possible;

2) I did not want him to be with me because he "needed" me, but because he "wanted" me;

3) even if we were in a relationship, I needed to see him stand on his own two feet, handling his own affairs consistently so that I could feel comfortable that if the situation ever arose in our relationship, he could take care of me;

4) I did not want to be used; and

5) I wanted him to provide a place for me that would be an escape from my normal surroundings. These were my

"fundamental laws," my bottom line as it were - in no particular order.

With those principles as my foundation for the decision, my decision became clear. The hardest part was the work involved in being honest enough with myself to admit my truths. It was difficult because I did not want to disappoint this man. I wanted to be there to support him. But, if the truth was to be told, I knew that there was a possibility that he would stay in my life longer at this time because he needed help. He did not come back into my life seeking help. The circumstances developed when his plans fell through. That produced the need. In making the decision, I had to set aside how he came to need me and look at what that now meant for me.

I had to decide what I was willing to offer in the way of assistance that would not – no matter what – allow me to be taken advantage of.

What made this a challenge for me is I discovered that I have a history of putting the needs of men ahead of my own in a relationship. This stemmed from my relationship with my father. In fact, this man's behavior was very similar to my father's. My natural instinct is to put aside my needs and wants for the benefit of the men in my life. It has led to hurtful outcomes. Just because I know this, doesn't mean that the tendency toward this behavior stopped. It is represented by emotions and insecurities that arise in a given situation. This one was certainly one of those.

It was a struggle to push that aside and to unravel what was important to ME. I had to set aside how he would feel about my decision. This was hard because I want to be in a relationship with him. I want him in my life. What changed in me was that I no longer wanted that more than I wanted to be at peace.

It is critical to note that once you know yourself, in particular, what your brand of crazy and unhealthy is, that you will still be confronted with those issues for many years to come. Think about it this way: if the behavior didn't develop over night – and it never does - it won't disappear over night. Becoming conscious of our unhealthy behavior requires work. Since you put in the work and now understand your unhealthy tendencies, that knowing does not mean you won't be tested.

I am certain, however, that in the process of discovering those unhealthy tendencies, you identify a pattern of behavior that you consistently engage in that leads to the same outcomes. In that, there are certain feelings that arise every time. Let's call those warning signals, like the construction worker with the slow/stop sign in the middle of the road. They will pop up. When they do, it is our responsibility to heed them. This is where you begin to ask the "why" questions. This is the beginning of the "why journey." This leads directly to the fundamental laws that will govern your conduct and honor your devotion to right.

Allow yourself time to honor your needs, wants and desires. You're worth it.

Once I got beyond my feelings, emotions, unhealthy behavior patterns and all of that, my choice was very clear to me. Now universal spirit law required me to verbally express that to this man. As my heart raced and my stomach turned, I told him what assistance I was willing to offer.

The principles, my fundamental laws, were not tangible, material things. They could not be seen with the naked eye. In fact, they were buried under my emotions and feelings. I had to dig for them. However, as invisible as they appeared, they proved to be the very substance of the entire exchange.

The principles are THE THING ITSELF. In other words, they are the only things that mattered. That space is where my truth lived. It was my safe zone. It was the space that protected me and offered me the best chance of coming out of the situation unharmed and most importantly, at peace.

If this circumstance was going to produce a healthy, long-lasting relationship with a man that I love and I know for sure loves me, I had to stand in the principles. I had to set boundaries for him and I had to base that on those principles. I would not set the boundaries based on my emotions and feelings toward him. I also would not set the boundaries in service to appearances. What do I mean by that? In society today, there is an unspoken belief that if you are single, you are less than. Only people in a relationship are valuable. If you are single, there is something wrong with you. Hopefully, no one will try to debate society's unspoken messaging.

In the situation I was facing, it would have been easy to allow a relationship to develop that would give the appearance that I was in a great relationship. Underneath that appearance could have been all sorts of unhealthy behavior. I was more concerned about the health of the relationship than its appearance.

So often people remain in unhealthy, unfulfilling relationships for appearance's sake. I long ago gave up caring about others' impressions of my relationship status. It was easy to do once I discovered how unhappy and unhealthy a lot of couples are.

Worse, I have discovered how long couples will stay together while being unhealthy and unhappy. I had learned in my youth that I was not willing to live an unhappy, unhealthy life just for the sake of appearances. I was not willing to give up my peace to avoid the shame of society for being single. It just wasn't worth the pain.

People make choices that factor in "what are they going to think of me?" This should be the least important element of anyone's decision-making process. Everyone will use a different path or process to make decisions. This book is to share with you the principles revealed to me in a very delicate situation. I have since realized that it is the most efficient way to make decisions for myself, or whatever entity for which I am positioned to make decisions. It worked in a romantic situation, it worked in a business situation and it works even when the decision is of marginal importance, like what to eat for dinner during the coronavirus pandemic.

I was simply tired of washing dishes three times a day during the stay-at-home order of the 2020 COVID-19 pandemic. It seemed to me that all I did was wash dishes. There came a day when I just didn't want to wash anymore dishes! So I made a

23

peanut butter and jelly sandwich for dinner. Sounds silly, right? Well, I knew myself enough to know that I did not want to wash any dishes that night. I did not give weight to the fact that I am a grown woman and was blessed to have a wide variety of healthy foods in the refrigerator that I could eat.

I did not give weight to the fact that if someone knew that I was too lazy to cook for myself, they might scorn me. I focused only on my bottom line – I was not washing dishes that night. I ate my peanut butter and jelly sandwich with great satisfaction. I didn't wash dishes that night, either.

The grand point here is that this method works in every category of decision-making. While the principle is invisible, it is THE THING ITSELF. It is the substance that must not be violated in every situation. Live the principle and not the appearance. The principle is the only stability and safety for our delicate feelings. It is the place that makes it safe to be vulnerable. It is also the place that minimizes making emotionally charged decisions. It minimizes DRAMA!

Focusing on the principle at play is also, as I have discovered, where I access my power most easily. Despite not being seen with the naked eye, principle is the source of all power to affect every situation. In fact, from a metaphysical, spiritual standpoint, principle is the pure power source. For those who believe in a higher power of any nature, you understand that your higher power is invisible. You seek that invisible place when you need comfort, mercy, grace or to give praise.

Well, it is also the place that we should all go when we need power to affect our daily lives. We should die daily to our own concepts (keep asking why we feel and believe what we believe in every situation) to live more fully in the ways of our higher power. That higher power is pure potential. Therefore, it provides options limited only by the principle at play in the moment. It will reveal options we did not think existed when we were weighed down with ancillary concepts like what will they think about me if I do or say this, how will they feel about my choice, will they still like me if I am honest with them about how I feel?

Once we die to those concepts, pure principle can open our eyes to options we did not know existed. I have found those options to be clearly available and the most productive.

The principle must always be the motivation behind all decisions. Anything else is on shaky ground. It may produce a healthy outcome or it might not. Remember, the place of principle is the place of safety and stability. When all is going crazy and looks chaotic, revert to the principle, the bottom line for you. It will clear away the noise long enough for you to remember what is most important to you and what is most likely to produce the outcome that works best for you. Others may not like it, but they will respect you for making the choice.

Even if they don't tell you at the time, they will respect you. Besides, you are not expected to live for other people's brand of crazy or chaos. You are not responsible for how they feel about the choices you make for yourself. We are responsible for the choices we make. If someone's feelings are hurt, we have to own that. It may be an unintended consequence of the choices we make when we are principle centered. However, I have found that I can accept those consequences better than the consequences I suffered when I made decisions centered on the feelings, needs and wants of others while my needs and wants were not met.

A major benefit to focusing on the principle and making the main thing the main thing is that it forces you to deal with the most powerful force in your life – YOU. For those who believe in something greater than yourself, it forces you to access that information source, that power to make your decisions. You will never go wrong accessing and utilizing your internal power source to make decisions to meet your needs, attain the desires of your heart or determine your position.

I am reminded of a sentence from the book "Jesus Always" by Sarah Young. This is a 365 day devotional book. It provides inspiration for each day of the year.

On July 10, the author refers to your soul as the "eternal part of you."

She goes on to say: "[I]t is the "real you" that is being transformed from Glory to Glory. Therefore, do not be discouraged by the defects you see in yourself. Instead remember that you are continually being transformed . . ."

When you interact and rely on principles, they are invisible, just as your internal, eternal power source is invisible. But know for a certainty, that it is the thing itself. It is the best access to power over your life that you have available to you. It will not depart from you. It will always be available to you in your time of need. It simply takes the courage to admit the TRUTH of what it says.

A word of caution: It is not always sweet and nice. It may reveal some really ugly truths about you. This is where the process gets difficult and why people often abandon the self work at this point. Nobody wants to admit that they are flawed, but everyone IS. Nobody is perfect, nor will anyone ever be perfect while in a body. The things we don't want to face are the very things that prevent us from living an authentic life and hiding behind excuses, deflections and projections onto other people.

This process prevents us from truly resolving anything. It causes us to compromise our truth for the sake of keeping the peace. It causes us to keep up appearances. I have done these things with terrible outcomes.

I remember allowing a man to monopolize all of my free time despite him telling me from the beginning that he did not want a girlfriend. I allowed him access to me as if I was his girlfriend without him having any responsibility to me as a boyfriend because my truth was that I believed, subconsciously, that if I did not, he would leave and the relationship would end. Guess what? It ended anyway. It ended because my failure to require anything for access to my time caused him to become subtly disrespectful of my time. It caused him to disregard my feelings and wants. He was always there when I needed him, but not when I wanted him to be there.

If I had made my wants a priority for him or me, maybe things would have been better. Maybe they would not have. The point is simply this: I let my needs, wants and desires go unexpressed in an effort to save the relationship and the very fact that I didn't require anything caused the relationship to end anyway. I suffered months of mental anguish, pain and humiliation for failure to be honest with myself about what I wanted. This was not the man's fault. The blame was all mine. Period.

Spend enough time determining your position based on principle so that when you have to live with the consequences you are in a safe place for yourself. Your principles don't have to make sense to everyone. If they are truly how you feel, it won't matter whether they are real or not.

A person's perspective becomes their reality. Until that perspective changes, a person will always behave as if their version of things is real.

By using the next step and verbalizing it to the other party, you may discover something that changes your perspective and may actually change your position. If you have based your position on principle, however, a shift in position will be easy to determine because you will have uncovered what your bottom line is. It is easy to know how new information fits into a solid principle.

STEP 2 TAKEAWAYS

1. The hardest part may be getting honest enough about your real feelings/needs/wants to bring your position to light.
2. Even after you "know yourself"- your brand of crazy or unhealthy – you will be tested with it.
3. The familiar uncomfortable feelings/emotions are a sign that it's time to start asking a series of "why" questions to uncover the actual principle at play because what you think is the principle at play may be a symptom and not the cause. The actual cause may be buried much deeper and is the very substance of your issue.
4. Principles are invisible, but they are the "thing" that MUST not be violated in every situation. Principles are the essence of what has to be decided.
5. Live the principle, not the appearance.

6. Universal spirit law is pure principle. Focusing on pure principles will reveal possibilities that you never thought of.
7. The place of principle is the place of stability and safety.
8. Principle gives you access to your internal power source. Using this transforms you from glory to glory.
9. If you ground your position in principle, when you gain new information, discover that you may have been incorrect about an underlying assumption it is easy to shift the demand without compromising your values because you have reached your bottom line and there is clarity in the principle.
10. Know what you will do if your conditions are not met.
11. All conditions must be realistic and achievable to be just.

VERBALIZE YOUR POSITION

Once you have thoroughly examined yourself, you know what principle(s) is(are) at play in the situation and determined your position, what I consider the most important step is Step 3 – you must verbalize your position, needs and expectations. This is, in effect, setting your boundaries. You have to verbally inform the others involved what your position is. That sets the boundaries and parameters under which you will engage in the situation.

It removes any confusion later when and if you have to mete out consequences for failure to perform. It is not justice to punish someone for something they didn't know was a punishable offense or failure.

This is the step many people skip or neglect either because they think the other party should already know or they're afraid that

31

the honest discussion will end the relationship or engagement, whether it's business or personal.

I can attest to the extreme anxiety I felt in having to speak - out loud - what my position was in offering help to the man I wanted to be in a relationship with but didn't want to take advantage of me. I was trying to balance my true desire and want of a lasting relationship with him with the following Fact's:

1. He had only recently reentered my life.
2. He had been inconsistent in his presence.
3. He was now in need.
4. I didn't know for sure if his interest in me at this time was more need than want.
5. I needed to see this man stand on his own two feet to feel confident that he would be able to take care of me in the future if necessary.

Fact 4 was the most delicate. It called into question his integrity. I didn't feel I could say that because it would have put him on the defensive. That would not have been an issue if I didn't really, really want the relationship. Since I did want the relationship, I was still concerned with whether I offended him or not. I could only imagine how it would feel on the other end.

My empathy was in overdrive. It was also complicated by the fact that I knew, for certain, no questions asked, that he loved me dearly. He always had. But that did not necessarily translate into him wanting to be with me. He had disappeared out of my life on more than one occasion in the past. We never fought or had disagreements that preceded the disappearances. He simply would just be gone. Sometimes for months. It had been about two years prior to this current reappearance.

How could I know, within a few months of "every couple weeks connections" whether he was here to stay? How could I know? I couldn't. I had experience with him popping in and out of my life without explanation. I had allowed it in the past. To be very clear, some of my challenges were due to my own old, underlying insecurities. These were the ones that I have overcome for the most part, but as with most people, under pressure, they resurface to test my resolve.

Another factor that made this delicate was that I was different. I had come to understand my worth in ways that I didn't previously understand. I learned that my company alone was worth effort on the part of any man who wanted to access it. My company alone had value. I also learned that if I didn't require anything for access to my company, not only was I shortchanging myself, the man would ultimately lose interest. The very thing I didn't want would happen anyway. Men are hunters and gatherers. They enjoy the chase. If there is no chase, they lose interest. They set about to find another conquest. At this time in my life and personal development.

I understood the value of putting my needs, wants and desires on the table and, at a minimum, getting what I wanted out of each encounter. For example, on one of his couple-week visits, I asked him to do something for me, which he did, and when it was done and he asked me to do something for him, I declined. I did not feel like it.

33

In the past, I would have felt obligated to do something he wanted merely because he had done something that I wanted. I realized that it wasn't necessary. I had a right to ask for something and give nothing in return sometimes. In my history, I was always trying to work to prove that I was not a user, but a genuinely good person.

The tragedy is that every man that I knew already knew that from the beginning. My qualities were evident to them from the beginning. In fact, those qualities were what sparked their interest in me from the beginning. I did not need to audition for their interest. What I came to know, during his absence, was that I did not have to continue to prove that I was worthy of his time, attention and love. As I said, there was never a question of his love for me. Anybody who ever saw us interact could see it. We had people tell us as much on more than one occasion throughout the years of knowing each other.

Despite the anxiety, I still had to verbally state my position. I had to have the uncomfortable conversation. Society is so focused on eliminating "uncomfortable" from our experience that we cut off communication and actual relationship.

Since humans are involved in relationships with other humans, none of us will ever live without feeling uncomfortable. It brings to mind my facilitation of a group at a halfway house on the subject of confrontation. When people hear the word confrontation, they automatically assume it is a negative inter-action. The definition is: to deal with in an honest and direct way. What is negative about dealing with something in a direct and honest way? Well, society does not value direct, honest communication. However, it is a necessary element of living authentically and gives us the best chance at having what we really want and need. It brings us peace.

The very thing that we run from is the thing that we need to get what we want. It is a trick of the opposition spirit that some call Satan. That spirit feeds the exact opposite of the truth. If we honor our truth, share that truth verbally, there is little room for anyone else that we are in relationship with to "misunderstand" our position.

I am aware that when we verbalize our position, we own it. This is another reason people don't want to say it out loud. Once I have, I own it and if I don't live up to it, I am exposed for not holding to my position. We will discuss this in more detail in a later chapter. But for now, it is important to acknowledge that once we verbalize our position, if the other party doesn't fulfill the need, doesn't live up to the understanding, doesn't meet our stated expectations, we are now faced with what to do about it.

Instinctively, we know that if someone is told, there is no ambiguity about what is expected and, even worse, we got verbal agreement, and if the other party doesn't live up to that, we are required to respond.

It boxes us into a clear-cut choice – stay or go. When the other party doesn't respond in the way that we want them or need them to, there must be consequences. Whether we kick those consequences down the road for a while or not, there are consequences. Every time we allow our wants, needs or desires to go unmet, we are denying who we are and not living an

35

authentic life. We are also teaching others that it is acceptable to fail to meet our needs.

Another reason that you must verbalize your position is simple: nobody is a mind reader. Nobody knows what you need unless you tell them. It is unfair to expect someone to guess what you are thinking. It is a gamble that they will get it right in every situation. Odds are that they won't. It is much simpler to just tell them. It is even bigger to get them to acknowledge – verbally – that they understand what you need.

All of this verbal stuff breeds accountability into the mix. Everyone is now accountable for their part in the exchange. This, again, is what society discourages, but what it needs more of. We need to be more accountable to ourselves first, then to the people who we love and then to the community and world thereafter.

The concept of getting the other party to verbally acknowledge your need, want, expectation or boundaries is key. It, alone, is what creates the accountability. Once the other person verbally acknowledges that they understand, then you can, in fairness, hold them accountable. It is totally unfair to later punish someone for an offense they didn't know was a punishable offense. They can hold you accountable as well should you change your position mid-stream. This is not to imply that you can't change your mind or position mid-stream.

What you are required to do at that point is to verbalize the change and get buy-in again. You must understand, however, that in negotiations (which is what these conversations in healthy relationships should be), the other party may choose not to accept the new terms. This is also why people avoid having these uncomfortable conversations. This is also what takes place over a period of time so frequently that people end marriages because they "grew apart." Since we want to avoid being disappointed, I am clear that building in accountability is scary.

I would venture to say that it is scarier than the next step – watching the behavior of others. We are good at watching others disappoint us and are willing to stay in bad relationships (personal and professional), hoping they will get better. We will stick it out in some hot mess for years but won't exercise the courage to have a single conversation up front to avoid the mess on the back end. We are willing to fight for something bad but not take a chance on having an uncomfortable conversation that could likely lead to our good.

Often, we know that the other person is not capable or willing to meet our needs or wants. We know it in our bones. We don't want to set them up to prove they are not capable and certainly we don't want to know that they are not willing to meet our needs or wants. If we do, then we are obligated to deal with it. We can no longer run from the truth that we have known and avoided. OK, don't throw the book away. I know that was painful. In fact, I'm going to let you sit with that one for a few minutes.

Go get a cold drink and ponder that for a little while. I'll wait. . .

Understand that this is the most nerve-wracking step to take. This is where all of your fears and insecurities will come out from under the sewer and attack you like a sewer rat! All of the things you don't want to happen (realizing the person just isn't that into you, the business idea you had may fall apart because the other party doesn't want to agree to your terms, etc.) will race through your mind with a quickness.

This will be especially true if you are practicing this for the first few times. If it is your attempt to develop new habits in your life, set new boundaries, turn over a new leaf, the OLD will hunt you to make sure you are really about that new life you claim to have. Even for a person like me who is quite vocal, this step was filled with anxiety.

I must say that once it was said – verbally – I felt a great sense of relief. It was like, OK, it's out there now, no turning back. Well, there – I said it. At least he knows where I stand. It's too late to take it back. It really IS how I feel. Then came a sense of power. I was free to express my point-of-view at any time in the future about that subject because I had already said it – verbally. It was liberating.

I wasn't in the shadows of my old insecurities. I was walking in the light of my truth. I wasn't afraid anymore. I wasn't afraid if he would stay or go. I had drawn my lines. They were clear and understood. No matter what happened from that moment forward, I had my say!

The point is, no matter what FEELINGS rise up when you are determining your position or even when you are preparing to or in the process of verbalizing your position/needs/expect ations/boundaries, keep moving through them. Remember, feelings are JUST feelings. Let me side-track for a second on "feelings."

One of the definitions of feeling is: often unreasoned opinion or belief. This tells us that our feelings are not always reasoned or based in rational thinking. More likely, they are not. They are often an opinion or belief. Nowhere in the definition did it say that they are FACTS. It also did not say that they are TRUE. The point being, just because you feel something doesn't make it real, factual or even true. Just like 90% of what we fear never happens.

I don't want to throw feelings out the door. They are often the first indication that there is some danger ahead. The key is to analyze the feelings why am I feeling this way, where did that come from, ultimately, the series of "why's" again. Identify the source of the feelings. In the decision-making process, they should be analyzed, but not become the foundation for the choices made. I feel it was unfair that I wasn't built with a flat stomach. OK! And? Exactly. So do a million other people. But what is that relative to? Not much. Its just a feeling. It has no basis in reality that I was – what? – entitled to a flat stomach. Sounds silly because it is silly.

Don't let what you feel take you off your path after you did all of the hard mental work to determine your position. If you have answered all of your "why" questions, you did a great amount of work that you should not allow feelings to derail before you verbalize your position/needs/expectations/boundaries. You owe it to yourself to keep moving despite what you feel. A new feeling is coming right behind that one. It is a much more positive feeling. Don't stop, keep moving.

While verbalizing your position can be scary, it ultimately brings about a great sense of peace, freedom and power. There is freedom in living and speaking your truth. There is freedom from fear of what will happen next that you no longer have to hold on to because you already did the most courageous thing by speaking it out loud. There is power in having a clearly defined position that you no longer have to hide from others. We somehow believe that if we don't state our needs, wants, expectations or boundaries that they don't exist. Not true. Those feelings keep reminding us that we are not in our place.

STEP 3 TAKEAWAYS

1. Verbalizing your position, telling the other party out loud what your position is, is JUST. It is unfair to punish someone for behavior they did not know was punishable. This is especially true if you are correcting behavior that you are allowed to persist in the past without correction.
2. If your position stems from a need to correct old behavior that was previously acceptable, it may trigger old insecurities that you thought were put to rest. These are tests of your resolve and learning.
3. Verbalizing your position will likely be an uncomfortable conversation. Society leads us to believe that we should not suffer an uncomfortable moment. No growth happens from a place of comfort. If you want change, it will require uncomfortable conversations and moments.

4. Once we verbalize our position, we instinctively understand that we own it. We understand that if the other party fails to meet our needs or expectations, we now are obligated to do something about it. This may mean the end of the relationship. We would rather avoid that choice so we don't verbalize.

5. We know every time we do not exact consequences for the other party not meeting our needs, we are teaching them that it is acceptable to fail to meet our needs.

6. We are willing to fight for something bad but not take a chance on having an uncomfortable conversation that could likely lead to our good.

7. Remember, feelings are JUST feelings. Don't let them stop you from verbalizing your position. Just because you feel something doesn't make it real, factual or even true.

WATCH THE BEHAVIOR OF OTHERS

For some, Step 3 (Verbalize Your Position/Need/Expectation s/Boundaries) will feel like the hardest step because many of us find it difficult to speak up for ourselves. This may have occurred because we were taught that children should be seen and not heard.

We may have been physically or sexually abused in childhood and made to keep the secret for fear of retaliation against us or other members of our family by the abuser. We may have grown up in a house where "good people" didn't make waves. There are a number of reasons why people come to the conclusion that speaking their mind, verbalizing their truth, is not an acceptable thing to do, even if it means that their needs go unmet.

I decided as a child, I can't even remember exactly how old I was when I decided this, nor do I have any particular event that I can think of that caused me to make a conscious decision that if I did not put in whatever work was necessary to keep a relationship going with my father, we would not have a relationship.

I remember a specific incident that I write about in my book HURT PEOPLE HIGHWAY, Identifying Unhealthy Elements In Relationships, where I distinctly felt and believed (whether true or not), that if I did not call my father to wish him a Happy New Year, he would never speak to me again. To this day, years after his passing, I still believe that to be true. I have no physical proof of it and I never asked my father any questions about that year. I remember him crying that night. We both cried. I am not sure why he cried and thanked me so much, but I cried because he cried. I was about ten or eleven years old.

I am sure the idea grew prior to that because when that New Year's Eve came, I had already put the belief into action. I had already begun the practice of making sure that I maintained a relationship with my father, even if my needs were not met. I assumed the responsibility. This was the mind of a child. It did not matter whether it was factually true. It only mattered that I believed it to be the case. Therefore, I acted upon my belief. This was true my entire life until my father's death in December 2013.

For people who have a deep-seated belief that speaking the truth or speaking up for themselves is not acceptable or that addressing a situation in a direct or honest way is negative or will lead to the very thing they don't want, that can be a very scary proposition.

However, Step 4 – Watching the Behavior of Others is likely the hardest of all the steps for one reason: YOU CAN'T CONTROL THE BEHAVIOR OF OTHER PEOPLE. This is where people who have felt out of control throughout their lives and developed a controlling behavior pattern will feel as though they are going to lose their minds. This will feel like drowning over and over again. In my head, I imagine this must be what the waterboarding torture tactic feels like. This is the wait-and-see stage.

Watching the behavior of others after you have verbally stated your position is scary for a couple of reasons. I have found it scary because I didn't want what I didn't want to be true to be proven true. I didn't REALLY want to know if I was being set up to be taken advantage of as opposed to the man, I was in love with wanting to be with me because he was finally ready. It felt like sitting and waiting for the other shoe to drop and my worst fears being realized.

Strangely enough, however, it was easier than putting my feelings to the side and knowing that I had never spoken my truth and eventually the truth would come out. The circumstances would dictate that I speak the truth. I knew for sure that the sooner I stated my position, the fairer it was to both of us. Maybe that is what pushed me along, the notion of being fair to him. Whatever moved me to action, I am so glad it did. In the end, there was no miscommunication between us about what I was and was not willing to do to assist him in his time of need.

By this time I had also come to realize that when I did not speak my truth in the past in favor of maintaining relationships, they ended just the same. In other words, me sacrificing my truth, keeping my mouth shut in the name of peace and maintenance of a relationship FAILED. The relationships failed and I was miserable.

In a few business instances, I discovered that the sooner people understand what my position is, the more time it gives them to formulate their response. During this behavior-watching time, I did not have to engage in multiple conversations, continue to restate my position or politics to encourage the outcome I was looking for. I stated my position.

If they performed "x," then I would respond in a particular way that was spelled out. If they performed "y," I would respond in a different way. Both potential responses were laid out upfront. It gave everyone information that they needed to determine how they would behave.

It was a lot easier to verbalize and wait in the business arena. I am sure that it is because the emotions weren't so personal. In the affairs of my heart, my emotions were vying to play a bigger part in the decision. I had to push emotions aside because they are a byproduct of feelings. As we discussed earlier, feelings are just that. They are often unreasoned opinions. In business, I wasn't so concerned with whether the relationship was going to be a life-long partnership. I was only concerned about what was in the best interest of the people that I was responsible for protecting as their employer.

In the business instance, the position I took was made clearer to me because I focused on the principle at play. Being principle-centered helps to clear out the noise and emotion, as well. Even in business, no one wants to be taken advantage of.

I have seen people struggle to reach a business decision because they were not focused on the principle or foundation of the business, but rather profits only. That translates to being "money centered." That meant that doing the right thing for the employees became harder to decide because it would potentially require the company to spend or even lose money for a time. Companies do lose money from time to time in their quest to make money. Companies must spend money to make money. If the leadership of a company is money-centered, they will have anxiety about spending and certainly losing money. This will lead to hesitation to let the money go.

Hesitation can be a terrible practice in business, particularly in a crisis. In personal affairs, it may not be as easy to determine if the behavior that followed the verbalization actually meets the need. Sometimes it will be crystal clear: did he take out the trash and bring home the money for groceries?

If the trash is no longer in the house and the groceries are in the cupboards, he met the needs. Easy call. If, on the other hand, the conversation is about whether or not she is putting her church ahead of the family too often and you need her to spend more quality time taking care of your needs, it may not be as clear whether the response is adequate.

Let's say instead of going to the church every time the doors open (Sunday service, Tuesday Bible study, Wednesday choir rehearsal, Saturday clothes giveaway), she now only goes to the church two days a week. She is spending the rest of the time reading a book or doing crafts at home. Did she meet the need/expectation or not? This is a decision only the person making their position/need known can answer.

If the truth of the demand was to stop her from having an affair with the deacon at the church, this may suffice. If the reason for the demand was to have more quality time with her, then maybe not. In either case, the person who made the demand is the only person who can decide whether their position/need/expectation or boundary has been honored.

This is where all of the work done in Steps 1 and 2 will serve you well. In Step 1, you asked yourself a series of "why" questions that led to identifying the principle that you are standing on in this particular instance. This led to your ultimate truth and the fundamental law that you perceived was being violated. If the behavior shift is not entirely what you had hoped, going back to the principle, the comprehensive and fundamental law, will certainly reveal whether the behavior change is enough to satisfy the need and whether you should continue in the relationship. The work done previously will reveal whether the rule or code of conduct has changed sufficiently to satisfy the need.

The principle will always remain the same. It has no temperature. It is neither hot nor cold. It will not waiver. It is invisible, but as unmovable and unwavering as anything you can see. The principle is the most sound place to put your confidence and trust. It is the safest place for your hopes and dreams. It is the unfailing arms of universal spirit law. No matter what the physical looks like, the principle will reveal whether it is true or not.

Remember that people can behave appropriately for a short period of time. Heck, in Heaven, Satan transformed into an angel of light. But it didn't last. For people in abusive relationships, the abuser becomes quite charming after an incident of abuse. When watching the behavior of others, we need to allow enough time for them to be consistent in the change. We also have to give credit for trying to meet our needs. Sometimes we are so rigid in our expectations that we don't allow room for human failures.

If a person is trying with everything, they have to accommodate your position, it should be given credit. That is NOT to say that just because they try that it should be enough to cause you to lower your standards. If the needs are not actually met and you have determined that you must have whatever it, is you asked for, then your only choice is to respond however you said you would if your need was not met.

There is a fine line between giving credit for trying and moving your boundary. It is only by holding the principle up that you will be able to determine which one you are doing. When we want something badly enough, we will try to justify the behavior of others to fit our narrative so that we are not required to take any action that we don't really want to take.

Speaking for myself, I could justify almost anything if I wanted to. If I could "understand why" someone behaved the way they did, then it was acceptable that they didn't meet my needs or disregarded my feelings. Poor thing. They were suffering and I was going to be all right. I could handle it until they got better or realized just how valuable I was to them. I wanted them to know how committed I was to them and their needs. That is fine for a while, but at some point, my needs had to be addressed.

My willingness to put my needs aside for a time became the norm. I was teaching people from the beginning that I was willing to put their needs first and forego my own. I did not set the expectations high enough for me to sustain a relationship. Then I would be hurt when I was depleted. It was my own fault. I had to teach people from the beginning that my needs had to be met.

It also gave a false impression to the person that I was in a relationship with that it would always be acceptable to disregard my needs. It gave the impression that the benefits they got in their relationship with me didn't come with a price. I realized that being with me was as easy as getting the local grocery store sales papers in the mail. It didn't require you to do anything. They just showed up. They were free.

Since I made all of myself available for the price of a weekly sales paper – free – I got treated like the weekly sales paper. What do we do with those? Sometimes we use them to wash windows, use them to pack fragile things during moving (this is most like how I was treated – LOL), and more likely than anything, ultimately, they are thrown in the trash.

WATCH THE BEHAVIOR OF OTHERS

I never had traditional low self-esteem. I always knew that I didn't deserve to be mistreated. I just didn't know how I should be treated. This was the product of not seeing a healthy intimate partner relationship in my household. My mother didn't bring men around my siblings and me until I was a teenager. I never knew what to require. She was clear that I was not to let anyone take advantage of me and certainly I was never to financially support a grown man. There was never to be physical abuse. So in some regards, I knew to protect myself from some things, but had no clue that I was being taken advantage of in other areas.

I would eventually begin to feel dissatisfied in the relationship.

Small disrespect always leads to larger disrespect over time. Because I required so little, over time, I got less. Ultimately, the relationships would end. Interestingly, it was usually me that ended relationships. As I think about it now, it makes sense. Of course I would end the relationship. The other person's needs were being met! I was a pretty low maintenance kinda girl. I had been raised and trained to be a woman. My mother was fond of saying I was raised and not drug up. That meant that I knew the things that women needed to know to sustain a household. I learned how to cook, clean, raise children, dress appropriately for any situation, manage finances and I enjoy sports and sex.

What else did a man want? They love the chase. I wasn't providing the chase.

Watching the behavior of others is the step where I felt most helpless. I could only watch to see if they would meet my needs. I could not control their behavior. It could also be a time of great anxiety for people that need to control things in their world. Often, people who grew up in dysfunctional homes will develop a need to control their environment and everybody in it. Since they felt so out of control as a child, as an adult their response is to control everything they can.

Watching the behavior of others for this person may trigger the feelings of helplessness. One thing I had to become comfortable with is that the other person may not meet my needs and once that became clear, I was in control of my own behavior. I was not a victim. Whether they met my needs or not, I was still in control of ME. That became a comforting thought for me. Since I had put in the work to understand the fundamental law that was motivating me, I knew what my next move would be if my needs were not met. I knew what came next. That provided comfort whenever the insecurity of the situation would arise.

One challenge during the watching stage was to balance enjoying the relationship while watching to see if my needs were being met. I had long ago learned that bad news travels enough; take time to enjoy the good times when they are available.

If I was constantly focusing on whether or not the person was addressing the concern I raised, I would run the risk of not being present and allowing myself to enjoy the good times that were happening. It can be challenging to focus on watching and living in the moment. I would always rest easier when I reminded myself that it was fine for me to have fun while it lasted. I deserved it. I had earned the fun. If and when it was made clear that my needs were not going to be met, that was when I had to change my behavior.

Notice, I did not say change the other person. The only person I can control is me. So at the moment it became clear that my need was not going to be met, that is when my behavior needed to change. It did not matter whether the other person didn't want to meet my needs or was incapable of meeting my needs. For me, the end result was the same. It was now up to me to choose whether to continue in the relationship or leave.

It may not always come down to ending the entire relationship either. It may simply be changing my behavior in that area of the relationship. It may be as simple as me no longer making this person a priority in my life. Maybe they only get back what they invest. The choice and control of what I offered was in my hands and mine alone. What I did once it was clear that my needs were not being met was totally my doing. I owned it and all of the consequences, good or bad.

In my personal relationship, the situation called for a deadline to be met. I had set a boundary – the deadline – and in my spirit I was adamant that it be met. I was clear that the date had to be met. I thought I understood why, during the watching period, it was so important that the deadline was not missed. However, after I enforced the deadline, and thus ended the relationship, I was shown what I write in this book and in particular, why it was so important to enforce the deadline.

If I had moved the deadline by even one day, I would have been teaching the man that my boundaries were soft. I would have been sending mixed messages. Later in the relationship, I would have become angry or hurt that he routinely disregarded my boundaries. It would have been my fault. I would have shown him through my actions that I didn't necessarily mean what I said. I didn't need what I said I needed. In effect, my word meant nothing.

Due to my obedience to the principle at play, I was spared being forced to extend myself way beyond what I wanted to. I may have been forced during the 2020 COVID-19 stay-at-home orders to shelter-in-place with someone with whom I did not want to live. It would have been a direct result of me moving my boundaries and sending mixed messages.

It has been said that we teach people how to treat us. I learned through this experience that if we declare that we must have a certain thing and settle for anything less, we are sending mixed messages and setting ourselves up for the other person to disregard our boundaries. That is not the other person's fault. It is our fault. We are the ones who showed them that our boundaries could be observed sometimes and sometimes not.

On a similar note, it is one of the main reasons that relationships that start by one or both parties cheating on their current significant other don't work over time.

Here's why. In the beginning of the relationship, each party knows that the other party is violating the relationship they are in. Even if one party is not violating their own relationship, they are willing to participate in violating the other person's relationship.

More often than not, neither of these parties ever trusts the other person because at the beginning, they showed that they were willing to participate in violating a relationship. They exposed a major character flaw to the other person. The character flaw is now part of the foundation of the relationship. You can't build a solid relationship on a faulty foundation. It just doesn't work that way.

There are no circumstances that justify cheating. It is not complicated. Either the two people are available to be in a relationship or they should wait until they are. The people involved never really trust each other because of how the relationship started.

Watching the behavior of others, giving them the opportunity to perform, meet your needs, fulfill a commitment can be hard for people inclined to doing everything themselves. It is the time when you should be doing nothing.

I have discovered for myself that doing nothing was the hardest thing I ever had to learn how to do. So I understand the challenge.

STEP 4 TAKEAWAYS

1. Step 4 may be scary because you have NO CONTROL OVER OTHER PEOPLE. All you can do is wait and see what they do.
2. The higher the quality of the work you put in on Steps 1 and 2 the better it will serve you in Step 4 because it will have revealed the principle you are standing on. Focusing on the principle in evaluating whether the behavior change has been sufficient will make it clear. If you focus on only the physical, you may find it difficult to decide if the behavior change is enough.
3. It may be easier to determine if the behavior change was enough in business as opposed to personal affairs. Affairs of the heart often come charged with emotions that are not necessarily involved in business.
4. Most people can change their behavior for a short period

of time. Whether they can change it consistently is another question. Only the person who has verbalized the need can determine whether the change is sufficient.

5. A person trying to meet your needs must be given credit. However, even if they make an effort and are given credit for making the effort, only the person that verbalized the need can determine if it is sufficient to stay in the relationship. Just because someone "tries" does not mean they have succeeded. You should not feel obligated to continue in any relationship just because they tried. In basketball, the team doesn't get a point because the player gave it his best shot and it didn't go into the basket.

6. There is a fine line between giving credit for trying and moving your boundary. It is only by holding the principle up that you will be able to determine which one you are doing.

7. Once it is clear that your needs are not being met, you must do something. Whatever you do, you own it and all of the consequences, good or bad.

8. If we declare that we must have a certain thing and settle for anything less, we are sending mixed messages and setting ourselves up for the other person to disregard our boundaries as long as we are in a relationship with them. We also set the other person up to fail us because the messaging is conflicting.

DO WHAT'S IN YOUR BEST INTEREST

Once you have watched the behavior of others and it is clear that they have not fulfilled your needs, met your expectations or are still violating your boundaries, it is time to adjust your behavior. It's your move. If you are certain that the behavior of the other entity involved has not been sufficient to resolve your issue, it is now time to implement the action steps that you decided in Step 2 – Determine Your Position.

If you fail to adjust your behavior in the way that you verbalized to the other entity, you have effectively shown them that you don't mean what you say. This will establish a pattern for all future dealings. Notice that what you have to do is "adjust your behavior." This is what you control. Everything in your life is about you, not others. You are responsible for and control your behavior.

58

DO WHATS IN YOUR BEST INTEREST

If you did sufficiently detailed work in Step 2, you will know exactly what performance looks like. You will know what time frame the performance should have happened within. You will have determined a reasonable method of evaluating performance.

In Step 4 – Watching The Behavior of Others, you should have been watching the behavior to see if the changes necessary were being made, the unwanted behavior stopped, if sufficient progress has been made toward an end that would take a longer period of time to completely correct.

Remember, the behavior you identify in determining your position and then require of others should be specific and realistically achieved. If the other person is incapable of performing (fulfilling your needs, meeting your expectations or honoring your boundaries), it is unrealistic to impose your position. You already know, after an unemotional, realistic evaluation of the situation, that they are incapable.

You have assessed the situation with a direct and honest eye. It requires confrontation to make Step 2 useful. You have focused on the principle at play.

It is why I believe Step 2 is the most important step. Step 3 – Verbalize Your position/Need/Expectations/Boundaries is the hardest for me, but the most important is Step 2 because this is where I decide what I am going to do. Step 2 is where I make an honest assessment of myself and the other entity involved. I ask enough "why's" to know for certain why I have decided to require specific behavior and, hopefully, have determined

59

the other party's realistic ability to perform by removing the emotions and focusing on the principle at play.

Step 2 is also where honest assessment of my motivation is required. It is easy to decide what someone else needs to do to make the situation work for you. It is critical to ask yourself what you are willing to give to have get what you say you want. The assessment must include what, if anything, you need to do differently to bring about the results that you seek.

A valuable lesson I learned as a result of the most painful relationship I had ever been involved in was that as long as I focused my attention on the behavior of the man, I never resolved my issue and the pain continued. Focusing on what he did in the relationship never revealed how he was put in position, BY ME, to do those things. It never revealed my underlying issues that caused me to participate in the things that brought me so much pain. It never revealed that I was the cause of the pain I was in.

While that was the most painful day of my life – let's face it, nobody wants to acknowledge that they played themselves and caused themselves so much pain – it was also empowering because I learned that day that "I" had the power to ensure that it never happened again.

I was in control of my behavior. I no longer had to participate in any relationship that was not fulfilling. I learned that some of the hurtful tactics that he used to control me were to cover his own insecurities and were the result of his own childhood issues.

There was never a time that my behavior would have produced the results I was looking for. This man had to want to make the changes necessary to fulfill my needs. More accurately with this particular man, he had to want to fulfill my wants. The man loved me and always made sure that my needs were met, but he was never available to fulfill my wants.

As long as I focused my assessment on him, I never healed. I had to admit something painful about myself to myself, but I gained valuable insight into why I behaved the way I did. It produced understanding and showed me my power to make sure it never happened again.

Focusing on the other person may appear to be easier, but in reality, it prolongs the drama and pain. It was imperative that I clearly understood what I was willing to give, offer, provide, BE, when determining my position and what assistance I could make available to the man I wanted to be in a relationship with.

I hear people discuss what they want to GET from a relationship, but not a lot about what they want to GIVE or BE in a relationship. In order for a relationship to be healthy, it must be balanced. No one party can receive all of the benefits.

In HURT PEOPLE HIGHWAY, Identifying Unhealthy Elements In Relationships, I explain in detail the elements of a "healthy relationship." In short, a healthy relationship is appearance and behavior indicating soundness and balance in a state of affairs existing between those having relations or dealings.

Why is this important? Words matter. Words convey thoughts.

Thoughts convey principles. As discussed earlier in this book, the principle is the thing itself. The principle is invisible but the safest place to reside. Also, the words used to define a healthy relationship give us language to understand what the interaction should look like in action.

Again, I must stress that this assessment must evaluate what you are willing to do, be or give toward the outcome. No one is a success alone, not in any endeavor.

A healthy relationship is no different. Whether it is business or personal, all relationships require balance and that it be rooted in a sound foundation. The sound foundation is simply truth and honesty. The most successful relationships in business are described as "win-win." This simply means that at the beginning of the negotiations to establish the business relationship, the parties all envisioned getting something they wanted.

Moving forward, the parties may not get all that they wanted and hoped for, but enough to keep them in the business relationship. All parties walk away with something they wanted. They all walk away with a win. In negotiations and subsequent relationships where all parties don't feel they got anything, there is usually underlying resentment that will surface again and again. It is because there was no balance.

If all parties did not convey their true self-interests or motivations, it was not built on a sound foundation and that lack of transparency will become apparent during the course of the business dealings.

Personal or intimate relationships work the same way. If, at the beginning, the parties don't negotiate the nature of the relationship, in detail and verbally, one party's needs are the focus or one party came into the relationship not being transparent, the operation or function of that relationship will eventually show that it was not built on a sound foundation. It will wobble. In order to get, you gotta be willing to give! You will find that when you are willing to give and, in fact, do give, that you will attract to you what you want to receive.

I have not had a significant other in a few years.

What has been interesting to me, however, is that there are men who I have met, we are not and have never been intimate, but they want to protect me, try to make my daily load easier and genuinely love, respect and appreciate me. I don't know about you, whether male or female, but I want those things in an intimate partner.

This brings to mind a point that I feel led to address. Go with me on this sidetrack for just a minute. Of the characteristics in the last sentence: making the load easier, provide protection, love, respect and appreciation, what makes men and women FEEL loved, is different. Almost without exception, women's highest desire in a relationship with a significant other is to feel "safe in their position." It makes her feel loved. For a man, his highest desire is to be "appreciated." It makes him feel loved.

What I learned through years of research in facilitating groups with both men and women is that these themes run through every relationship. If the man does not feel appreciated for the things that he does, he is discontent. If a woman doesn't feel safe in her position with her intimate partner, she is discontent.

Each may stay in the relationship hoping that someday the person receiving their affection and dedication will recognize that their actions are all to show their love toward them. In reading the book The Five Love Languages, written by Gary Chapman, I discovered that the biggest reason that relationships fail is that we tend to love the object of our affection IN THE LOVE LANGUAGE THAT IS MOST IMPORTANT TO US and NOT THE LOVE LANGUAGE THAT IS IMPORTANT TO THEM.

I felt it necessary to capitalize that information because I found that I was unknowingly guilty of showing love in a language that would make me feel love but it may not have been speaking to my partner.

Let me give you one of the most common examples I have seen since reading the book. Men are protectors and providers by nature. They often feel discontent, misunderstood or even dejected when they work really hard to provide a roof and necessities to their woman. Their every move in business is made with the family's needs and wants in mind. They put up with a world that beats them down every day just to provide for their family.

In this process, they are never home, they don't take vacations, when they are home, they are too tired to actually engage with the family and they don't understand why their marriage failed. It is because women need the attention of their intimate partner to feel safe in their position and thus loved. Feeling that a man loves and wants to be around her makes her feel safe. While provision is important to women, if she does not feel that he loves her, she will often not feel that her needs are being met.

On the flip side of that coin, a woman may do everything she can to show her man that she loves him by providing a well-run household.

However, if she fails to show him that she appreciates all of the hard work that he puts in to provide for and care for the family, he will not feel the same enthusiasm for her over the years because, in short, she is not speaking to him in the language that makes him feel loved. Read and re-read this until you understand it. This tidbit is worth the cost of the entire book. And I gave it to you for free! Oh, it isn't free, you already paid for the book. Whatever! Women want to feel safe in their position because it makes them feel loved. Men want to be appreciated because it makes them feel loved.

No matter what else you give to your significant other, remember to provide those elements. Without them, the relationship may last for years, but each will always feel something is missing. The need for those feelings are so strong in both sexes that failure to get these things at home makes a partner vulnerable to the seduction of someone on the outside who knows and is willing to provide what you will not.

It is not justification, but it is TRUTH.

What is in your best interest will vary depending on the

situation. It will also require different responses appropriate to the circumstances. It is important that the same response is not used in every situation. Typically, you think a hammer and nail go together. They do. What will change is which end of the hammer is used for the job in front of you. If you are constructing something, you use the round or square part of the hammer. If you are destructing something you use the other end to remove the nail. In either case, you are using the hammer.

The difference is in which end of the hammer is appropriate for the task at hand. Likewise, doing what is in your best interest may take on various forms.

- Stop certain behavior
- Start new behavior
- Reduce interaction
- End the relationship
- Replace a service provider
- Change the amount and type of interaction
- Look for new employment

Any of these may be an appropriate response to the behavior of others after you have verbalized your position. The good thing is that if you decided what the consequences or change needed to be in Step 2, you don't have to think about what comes next.

Sticking to your guns might make the other party uncomfortable, unhappy or angry as hell. It doesn't matter. If you instituted Step 3 as you should have out of sheer fairness, they should know that whatever you DO in Step 5 was coming. It should not be a shock to anybody involved that you are taking the actions that you are.

They may not like what you do, but they have no choice but to respect it. You were direct and honest with them about what your/position/needs/ expectations/ boundaries were. They had the opportunity to avoid whatever the consequences are at this point. They were in control of the one element you could not control – them. It is pretty difficult to play the victim when you controlled the outcome.

It will be especially shocking and enraging to a person who you have previously allowed to trample your boundaries, disappoint you, fail to live up to commitments they have made to you, take advantage of your skills and talents to their advantage while disregarding your well-being. In short, if this is new behavior in your interaction with this person/entity, it will come as a shock to their system and they will be even more offended because they are used to you behaving in a different way.

You may become unpopular in a circle of people because of your new process and directness. In today's times, in particular in 2020 in the United States, with a man in the White House who lies daily, the country is subjected to falsehoods regularly, even in dire circumstances, and it has given some the impression that truth doesn't matter.

From a spiritual standpoint, The Creator of Heaven and earth declared himself to be "the truth" and of course the opposition spirit will reject the truth. From a secular standpoint, society has moved further away from telling the truth and closer to saying what is convenient at the time or avoiding hurting someone's feelings or offending some group.

I strongly believe that the best place to land on this topic is in the truth. No matter how people feel about the truth, it is what it is. It has no temperature. As my wise friend Marlan says, "It is neither hot nor cold." It just IS. Avoiding the uncomfortable truth or inconvenient truth is a massive job. It requires mental manipulation of a person's own mind. The tragedy is that the truth is always apparent to everyone watching. It is always the elephant in the room. No amount of deflecting or screaming a lie over and over will change the truth. It is unmovable.

The truth is steadfast and unmovable because it is pure principle in operation. Remember, the principle will always remain the same. The situation, appearance or circumstances involved may change, but the principle at play will always remain when the dust settles.

The reason for this is that the ULTIMATE SOURCE AND SUBSTANCE OF ALL THINGS declared Himself/Itself/Herself to be the TRUTH. In fact, for those who read the Bible, in John 4:24 John writes, "They that worship Him MUST worship Him in spirit and in TRUTH." (Emphasis added.) That means that if you are a person who professes to worship the Creator described in the Bible, you MUST worship him in spirit and truth. Society does not operate according to the principles in the Bible.

Despite some in America professing that America is a "Christian nation," the reason the founders separated from England was for religious freedom. The founders specifically established a separation of church and state. That is their language, not mine. What is even more interesting is that the people that profess the most stringent religious leanings support the least religious behaviors toward their fellow human beings.

The one thing that is not on the above list is to RETHINK YOUR POSITION. At this point, you must take the action that you established. This is why it is so important to spend the time necessary in Step 2 to determine what you will do if the other entity does not perform in a satisfactory way.

You need to know exactly what you will do.

Once it is made clear that your needs will not be met, it is time to put into motion the action you planned and told the other party you would take. This is necessary for your word to mean anything in the future. We will discuss this in more detail later.

When you practice these five steps, you will find that you are a lot less stressed, you get what you need, your expectations are more often met because people have a clear sense of what they are and your boundaries will less likely be violated because you are not perceived as someone who will tolerate it. People will respond to you differently.

For some, this may not be a welcomed change in your behavior because they have benefited from your previous behavior. Some people may even become angry and no longer want to be in relationship with you. The person who borrowed money and never paid it back on time may no longer ask to borrow money from you because you set a firm date for repayment, took something they valued as collateral, verbally agreed to the date and explained that if they did not repay the money on time you were going to sell the item.

When they didn't repay on time, but a day later, the item was already sold.

Inevitably they will scream bloody murder. They will even argue that you were unreasonable because you "knew" they were good for it. You know they always pay eventually. The operative word in the last sentence is "eventually."

Well, that may be true and they had become accustomed to you waiting for your money. However, you need not feel bad for sticking to the deal. Again, they may not like it, but they have to respect it. An additional benefit is they may STOP borrowing from you. That can't be all that bad.

Another benefit to following these steps is that if one party in a transaction or relationship is going to be upset, I believe it's best that it not be ME. Call me crazy. I'll take that. I just don't want to be stressed and angry or disappointed. I may be disappointed once or twice with a person, but after that, if I put myself in the same position with that person again, it is MY FAULT. It is no longer the other person's fault for disappointing you when they have done it multiple times – twice is more than enough times – and you position yourself to allow them to do it again.

My mother had a lot of sayings. One of them was: "If you find a sucker, lick it!" Well, if I continue to put myself in the sucker position and you lick me, how can I be angry? I should only be angry with myself. The biggest benefit to following these five steps is that you live authentically. It reduces to almost zero the times you have to play along with others. These steps ensure that others know where you stand and you become known for being a straightforward person.

Clearly, in today's times, that is not necessarily rewarded with great fanfare or joy but if somebody's going to be upset, I'm always voting for the other guy. It is simply less stressful to have told the truth up front. In my circumstances with the man I love and wanted to be with, when he was not happy that I held to my position, I did not care. I had been totally honest about what I was willing to offer by way of assistance. We had an understanding that was verbally discussed on more than one occasion. I was not required to do anything else. If he wanted another agreement, it was HIS responsibility to say that.

It brings me to another point. When you verbalize your position, the other person may want to take the terms with conditions. If you are willing to adjust your position at that point, it is acceptable as long as you are not violating devotion to your fundamental law or code of conduct, the principle at play.

The longer they go on, the more relationships are a series of negotiations. People and circumstances change. The agreements we make today may not work in five years or even five months from now. When we discover this is the case, it is our obligation to the person that we are in a relationship with to verbalize again and reach a new agreement. It is crucial to note that the other person may not want to renegotiate. If that is the case, you have to know what you will do in that instance. If you always follow the steps, you should go into the negotiations with your position clearly thought out and what you are willing to give, be, do or not do before the conversation. The steps don't change, only the topic.

At this point in the steps, I have found that people who were accustomed to me not insisting on clarity and following up on agreements were angry. Some even ended the relationship. I have seen it work the same way with others. It is safe to say that some people will be angry enough to end the relationship. If that is the case, I have also discovered that it is for the best. Always remember that some people come into our lives for a reason, some for a season and some for a lifetime.

Everyone is not intended to be in our lives forever. If the person is an intimate partner, it may feel very hurtful. They did you a favor by exposing, sooner rather than later, that they do not want to be the kind of partner that you REQUIRE.

It is important for both males and females to require something of their partner. It keeps the relationship in balance, which is one of the fundamental elements of a healthy relationship.

The message you send when you don't follow through with your position is that your word means nothing. It sends the message that your boundaries are soft and your needs don't necessarily have to be met. You teach anyone in a relationship with you that your position in any situation is flexible. The result of this is that people selectively provide what you require.

It produces great frustration in your life.

The worst part is that YOU TOLD THEM IT WAS OK. You established that sometimes you mean what you say and sometimes you don't. You are actually being unfair to those people who want to be in relationship with you. You set a standard that abiding by your wishes is optional. It puts them in a position to choose when to honor your boundaries. It also puts them in a position to have to decide if this is a hard boundary or a soft one. Human nature dictates that people will assume in their favor.

People will generally do what is easiest or best for them in any given situation. In relationships, this means that sometimes they will do what is right by you and sometimes they won't. You will become frustrated and feel unappreciated, but it will be your fault. You have given them a choice that they are not qualified to make. Only you can decide which of your boundaries are firm.

The practice of selectively moving the finish line sends mixed messages that most people are not able to successfully read consistently. This produces the mixed responses that make us feel unappreciated and misunderstood. Again, this is our fault for sending the mixed messages. I never knew that I would be sending the message to my love interest that my needs only needed to be met sometimes and maybe not at all by doing something as simple as not holding him to a deadline.

This was a huge revelation to me. It explained so many of my past experiences. It is relevant to mention here also that if

73

you have not verbalized your position and been consistent in demanding that it be honored, the other party may be caught totally off guard by the severity of the punishment you mete out in a given situation because they have previously been allowed to disregard your boundaries. It is unjust to hold someone accountable in a severe way for something that you have allowed in the past WITHOUT VERBALIZING that this time is different. The reason it is different is not as important to verbalize as the reality that it is different.

If this is a relationship that you want to maintain, personal or business, you owe it to the other party to confront the situation. It gives them the opportunity to respond based on their level of commitment and interest in the relationship. This will give you a clear indication how valuable being in relationship with you is to them. This is valuable information to have when deciding whether to be in a relationship with someone.

Too often, I have seen people hold people accountable for things they never knew they were responsible for. A woman will withhold sex from a man because he didn't attend a social function with her. She never expressed that it meant that much to her. Sometimes he attends social events with her and sometimes he doesn't. This one was really important to her, but she never told him. When he said no, she simply sulked and simmered in her anger so that the next time he wanted to have sex, she had a headache. Now he's not happy.

A man will withhold his praise of his wife's efforts to make him an elaborate meal because she didn't have sex with him. He doesn't know why she didn't have sex with him. She doesn't know why he never said she did a good job when he knows how much that means to her. It can be a vicious cycle because neither is living authentically and verbalizing their need to the other.

The bottom line is a lot of pain and hurt can be avoided if people simply verbalize their needs/expectations/desires/boundaries. It is unfair to punish someone for something you never told them was a punishable offense.

STEP 5 TAKEAWAYS

1. The behavior you identify in determining your position and then require of others should be specific and realistically achieved.
2. Business or intimate relationships work the same way. If, at the beginning, the parties don't negotiate the nature of the relationship, in detail and verbally, one party's needs are the focus or one party came into the relationship not being transparent, the operation or function of that relationship will eventually show that it was not built on a sound foundation.
3. What makes men and women FEEL loved, is different. Almost without exception, women's highest desire in a relationship with a significant other is to feel "safe in her position." It makes her feel loved. For a man, his highest

desire is to be "appreciated." It makes him feel loved.

4. What is in your best interest will vary depending on the situation. It will also require different responses appropriate to the circumstances. It is important that the same response is not used in every situation.

5. People may not like what you do, but they have no choice but to respect it. If you followed Steps 2 and 3, you were direct and honest with them about what your/positio n/needs/expectations/ boundaries were. They had the opportunity to avoid whatever the consequences were at that point.

6. They were in control of the one element you could not control – them. It is pretty difficult to play the victim when you controlled the outcome.

7. The one option that is not available is to RETHINK YOUR POSITION. At this point, you must take the action that you established. If you don't, you will be violating yourself and there are severe consequences to you for doing that since your body is the temple of the Holy Spirit. You are also violating your power source.

8. Adjusting your position once the other party clearly under-stands your position and has not responded appropriately, sends mixed messages and sets you up for disappointment and sets the other party up to selectively address your requirements or needs.

9. It is unjust to punish someone for behavior that you have previously permitted without confronting it verbally. You have effectively set them up to FAIL YOU.

10. It is unfair to punish someone for an offense they never knew was a punishable offense.

Conclusion

~~~

IT WORKS IN EVERY SITUATION

Throughout this book I have tried to impart that this method applies to every situation. It works in your favor in every situation. It doesn't matter if it is an intimate partner, business, subordinates, supervisors, friendship, siblings, parents or children, it works in every situation.

The degree to which you have to work on Steps 1 and 2 may vary, but you will be using the same steps to be direct and honest and remain at peace. You may not be liked in the final analysis, but if you being at peace with yourself and your choices is important to you, then this method is for you.

The largest impact this method has had on my relationships of all kinds is that I am living authentically. The people that I engage with on any level know exactly whom they are dealing with. They know what to expect from me. Even if they don't like it, they respect me for letting them know up front.

This is a true blessing. I don't have to figure out ways to get what I need without actually speaking my truth. It also takes pressure off other people because they don't have to work so hard to figure out how to interact with me.

I can be corrected if I misunderstand something that I believe is truth. I am not overwhelmed with trying to be responsible for things I have no ability to control. I am only accountable for my part.

I am accountable to verbalize my position/need/expectation /boundaries and they are responsible for how they respond. This places my burden solely on me. It places the other party's burden squarely where it belongs – on them. So often when we try to anticipate and navigate the other party's response or feelings about our choices, we become overwhelmed because we are focusing on the wrong thing.

The reason we become overwhelmed is because we are out of order. We are now in someone else's lane. We have assumed responsibility for something that we have no control over. Whenever we attempt to manage something that is out of our control, we will have anxiety. That anxiety is an internal message that you are entering a danger zone.

It is futile to try to control things that are not in your power to control. The popular Serenity Prayer asks that the person praying be granted the power to accept the things they cannot change, the courage to change the things they can, and the wisdom to know the difference – all through a higher power. Sayings, phrases and clichés exist because they have stood the test of time, having been proven in a variety of circumstances.

In short, they are based in principle and therefore transcend the situation. They are universal laws that apply to most everyone.

Those sayings are repeated generation after generation because they are true principles. Remember that being "principle-centered" is the safest place to be. This is the ark of safety and peace.

It is clear to me that a major challenge to using the steps is that society has moved away from speaking the truth. It has become impolite to speak the truth without trying to soften its edges. In this year, 2020, in the United States of America, we have a president who is known more for being a liar than a leader during the time of a global pandemic.

Those that support him perform extreme twists and turns to justify supporting a man who they know, without any doubt, lies to their faces routinely. What is called "cancel culture" also exists in 2020. Society will cancel anyone out for being offensive to someone or some group. Comedians, who are normally applauded for telling the uncomfortable truth about someone in a funny way, are being shamed and losing their jobs for telling the truth as they see it.

People are taught as children that if they are too honest, they are rude. The word confrontation has a negative connotation. The reality is the definition is to address something in a direct and honest way. How can that be negative? It is very much considered negative in today's society.

With this backdrop, the steps may present a challenge to the person using them. It will especially be true in cases where the person using the steps did not previously stand their ground in their relations with others. It will be a shock to the system of those who became accustomed to the person not standing up for anything. They will likely become offended and angry.

Using the steps places a mirror in front of everyone to realistically look at the nature of their dealings. It requires looking at oneself with an honest eye to identify what it is that they stand for. It requires focusing on one's values and then fighting for them. It requires vocalizing to another person where you believe they have not met your expectations or needs. These kinds of conversations are never comfortable. They are especially difficult to have with people who have difficulty admitting that they have made mistakes.

The irony is that these are the people who will require use of the steps most often. They force you to have to assert your boundaries because they habitually violate them. It will be uncomfortable at first. It will get easier the more it is practiced. The difficult people will get used to it. They may never like it, but they will adjust. If they are meant to be in your life, they will adjust.

On the other hand, the greatest benefit of using the steps is that you live your life in the most authentic way. You live your truth more often. It is no longer necessary to run from the truth. With practice, you become skilled at verbalizing without attacking the character of the other party. It is important to note that it requires skills developed over time and with repetitive use to avoid destroying every relationship with people who aren't used to honesty while living authentically.

People will have no choice but to respect you for your position. No one likes a person who doesn't stand for anything. A person whose values shift with the situation can't be trusted.

Living in our truth gives others courage to live in their truth. It is time to get away from a phrase coined by Kellyanne Conway of the Donald Trump administration: alternative facts. It was astounding that she sat on national television with a straight face and used the term alternative facts as if it is really a thing. Facts are facts. As mentioned earlier, phrases that become clichés have stood the test of time.

One that has been used in recent years out of necessity is a quote by Daniel Patrick Moynihan: "You are entitled to your opinion. But you are not entitled to your owns facts." Facts are pesky things. They stand up under scrutiny; they stand up to lies. When we, as people, develop the habit of sticking to the facts, we too will stand up under scrutiny and pressure to lie. It becomes easier. In fact, it is a position I am most comfortable in.

I am so accustomed to people being uncomfortable with me telling the truth. The sad part is that once I speak the truth, others who did not have the courage to speak the truth are relieved. They may even chime in that they feel the same. Cowardice is one of my pet peeves. It annoys me that people are more concerned about appearances, peer pressure as adults or getting along with people they perceive to be in power than doing what is right.

Being principle-centered gives me the strength to do what is right, no matter the consequences. I am often labeled as hard or difficult because I will speak openly about what is true and what is in the best interest of the people I am serving.

There are power brokers in community development work that don't want poor people and certainly not minorities to have anything. People find it hard to believe that there are wealthy people that have more than they need, but are in opposition to poor communities having anything to serve them or make their lives comfortable.

I have experienced it firsthand in trying to provide for my community of African American and Latino people. There are organizations that claim to care about the needs of the people, but in reality, they just want to make money off the misery of the people.

They don't want to empower them to do for themselves. They don't provide services that will assist the people in becoming independent of them. Decisions that I make in my work are always about what is best for the people that I serve.

This became very clear to me during the 2020 global coronavirus pandemic. As an employer, there was no question whether I would adjust how we do business to protect the health of my coworkers. My friend works for a firm that is money centered. They waffled about whether and how to have their employees work from home because the truth was the leadership didn't want the staff to be able to "get paid for doing nothing.

I trust that my coworkers are going to do what needs to be done to keep their paychecks coming and appreciate me protecting their health. This firm was more concerned about the money and it made their decision more difficult.

They finally gave in when our state government issued a stay-at-home order. Had they cared about their employees and the right thing to do, there would have been no hesitation in moving their employees to a work-from-home scenario. They created anxiety in their employees through their slowness in making a decision and communicating it to their employees.

It is easier to decide the "right thing to do" when you focus on the principle at play. The principle will guide you to the right thing every time. It may not be popular and you may not be liked because of it, but it will be the right thing to do. I know that I have done the right thing or made the right choice when I feel a sense of peace. I may be facing backlash and have lost relationships, but if I feel calm inside, I know that I have done the right thing. It always comes to light later that I have done the right thing, despite how it looks early on.

The most precious gift I have is peace of mind/a sound mind.

Conclusion

That peace is not available as a sacrifice for any relationship. Focusing on principles and being guided by them keeps me in peace. That is why I fight to live by principles. They don't change. They are constant. The steps need to be used in every situation of importance.

This is not a one-time practice.

It is a way of living consistently that keeps drama to a minimum. I hope that by employing the steps you will come to know the peace of living authentically you – out loud.

www.ingramcontent.com/pod-product-compliance
Lightning Source LLC
Chambersburg PA
CBHW071418040426
42445CB00012BA/1199